THE ONLINE HUSTLE

A Step-by-Step Guide to Making Money Quickly and Easily on the Internet

By

Benedict Arnold

Contents:

Introduction:

- Why making money fast online is possible
- The benefits of making money fast online
- The potential risks and pitfalls to watch out for

Chapter 1: Identify Your Skills and Interests

- How to identify your skills and interests
- Matching your skills and interests with online opportunities
- Evaluating the profitability of your chosen online niche

Chapter 2: Online Marketplaces

- Overview of popular online marketplaces for freelancers and entrepreneurs
- How to create a profile that stands out

- Finding and bidding on projects that align with your skills and interests

Chapter 3: E-commerce

- Setting up an e-commerce website
- Product research and selection
- Creating and implementing a marketing strategy for your e-commerce business

Chapter 4: Affiliate Marketing

- Understanding affiliate marketing
- Finding profitable affiliate programs
- Creating content that drives traffic and conversions

Chapter 5: Online Investing

- Understanding the different types of online investment opportunities
- Evaluating the risks and rewards of online investing
- How to get started with online investing

Chapter 6: Online Courses and Coaching

- Identifying your area of expertise
- Creating and marketing your online course or coaching program
- Building and nurturing your online audience

Chapter 7: Freelancing

- Understanding the different types of freelance work available online

- Creating a standout profile and portfolio
- Finding and applying for freelance jobs

Chapter 8: Passive Income Streams

- Understanding passive income and how to generate it online
- Examples of passive income streams
- How to create and market your own passive income stream

Chapter 9: Tips and Tricks for Making Money Fast Online

- Time management tips for maximizing your earnings
- Common mistakes to avoid
- Staying motivated and persistent in your pursuit of online wealth

Conclusion:

- Recap of the strategies and methods covered in the book
- Final thoughts on making money fast online
- Encouragement to take action and get started on your online earning journey

Introduction

The internet has opened up a world of opportunities for those seeking to make money fast online. With a laptop and an internet connection, anyone can potentially earn a living online, and many have already done so. However, the world of online earning can be both exciting and daunting. On one hand, there is the potential for incredible financial rewards and the freedom to work from anywhere in the world. On the other hand, there are numerous pitfalls and scams that can lead to frustration, disappointment, and financial loss.

This book, "How to Make Money Fast Online," aims to guide you through the maze of online earning opportunities, helping you to identify the most lucrative and trustworthy methods of making money online. We will explore various strategies, from online marketplaces to e-commerce, affiliate marketing, online courses and coaching, freelancing, and passive income streams. We will also discuss the importance of time management, persistence, and avoiding common mistakes in pursuit of online wealth.

Whether you are a seasoned entrepreneur looking to expand your online earning potential or a beginner just starting out, this book will provide you with the knowledge and tools needed to make money fast online. So, let's dive in and explore the exciting world of online earning!

Chapter 1

Identify Your Skills and Interests

When it comes to making money fast online, one of the most important factors to consider is your own unique set of skills and interests. Identifying these can help you to match them with the most profitable and rewarding online opportunities. Here are some steps to help you identify your skills and interests:

Step 1: Brainstorm your skills - Make a list of all the skills you possess, from technical skills like web development and graphic design to soft skills like communication and leadership.

Step 2: Assess your strengths and weaknesses - Consider which skills you excel at and which ones you could improve upon. Knowing your strengths can help you to focus on opportunities that align with them, while identifying weaknesses can help you to determine areas where you may need to seek additional training or support.

Step 3: Identify your interests - Think about the things that you enjoy doing in your spare time, your hobbies, and your passions. Identifying your interests can help you to find online opportunities that you find fulfilling and enjoyable.

Step 4: Research online opportunities - Once you have identified your skills and interests, research online opportunities that align with them. Look for opportunities that match your skills and interests, and that also have a proven track record of profitability.

By identifying your skills and interests and matching them with the right online opportunities, you can increase your chances of making money fast online while also doing work that you find rewarding and enjoyable. In the next chapter, we will explore online marketplaces and how you can use them to find work that aligns with your skills and interests.

Chapter 2

Online Marketplaces

Online marketplaces are platforms that connect freelancers and entrepreneurs with businesses and individuals in need of their services. They provide a convenient and efficient way to find work, and they offer a wide range of opportunities for those seeking to make money fast online. Here are some steps to help you make the most of online marketplaces:

Step 1: Choose the right platform - There are many different online marketplaces to choose from, each with its own unique features and user base. Research different platforms to find one that aligns with your skills and interests.

Step 2: Create a standout profile - Your profile is your first impression on potential clients, so it is important to make it stand out. Use a professional profile picture, include a clear and concise description of your skills and experience, and highlight your best work.

Step 3: Find and bid on projects - Once you have created your profile, start looking for projects that match your skills and interests. Read the project descriptions carefully and make sure you understand the client's needs before submitting a bid.

Step 4: Communicate effectively - Communication is key to building a successful freelance career on online marketplaces. Respond promptly to client messages, be clear about your availability and pricing, and ask questions to ensure you understand the project requirements.

Step 5: Deliver high-quality work - Delivering high-quality work on time is essential to building a positive reputation on online marketplaces. Take the time to understand the client's needs, and provide regular updates on your progress to ensure that they are satisfied with the work.

Online marketplaces can be a great way to find work and make money fast online. By choosing the right platform, creating a standout profile, finding and bidding on projects, communicating effectively, and delivering high-quality work, you can build a successful freelance career on online marketplaces. In the next chapter, we will explore e-commerce and how you can use it to make money fast online.

Chapter 3

E-commerce

E-commerce refers to the buying and selling of goods and services online. It has become increasingly popular in recent years, and it provides a great opportunity for entrepreneurs and business owners to make money fast online. Here are some steps to help you make the most of e-commerce:

Step 1: Choose a profitable niche - One of the most important factors to consider when starting an e-commerce business is choosing a profitable niche.

Research different niches to find one that aligns with your skills and interests and that also has a proven track record of profitability.

Step 2: Build your online store - Once you have chosen your niche, it is time to build your online store. You can use platforms like Shopify, WooCommerce, or BigCommerce to create your online store quickly and easily.

Step 3: Source or create products - Whether you choose to source products from suppliers or create your own products, it is important to ensure that they are high-quality and meet the needs of your target audience.

Step 4: Drive traffic to your online store - Once you have built your online store and sourced your products, the next step is to drive traffic to your website. You can use a variety of strategies, including search engine optimization (SEO), social media marketing, and paid advertising, to attract potential customers to your online store.

Step 5: Optimize your sales funnel - To maximize your sales, it is important to optimize your sales funnel. This includes optimizing your product pages, creating effective product descriptions, and using upselling and cross-selling strategies to encourage customers to buy more.

E-commerce can be a highly profitable way to make money fast online. By choosing a profitable niche, building your online store, sourcing or creating high-quality products, driving traffic to your online store, and optimizing your sales funnel, you can build a successful e-commerce business. In the next chapter, we will explore affiliate marketing and how you can use it to make money fast online.

Chapter 4

Affiliate Marketing

Affiliate marketing is a popular way to make money online by promoting other people's products or services and earning a commission on any sales that you refer. It is a great way to make money fast online without the hassle of creating your own products or managing your own inventory. Here are some steps to help you make the most of affiliate marketing:

Step 1: Choose the right affiliate program - There are many different affiliate programs to choose from, so it is important to research different programs to find one that aligns with your skills and interests.

Step 2: Build your audience - To be successful in affiliate marketing, you need to build an audience of people who are interested in the products or services you are promoting. You can use a variety of strategies, including social media marketing, content marketing, and paid advertising, to attract potential customers to your website or social media platforms.

Step 3: Promote products effectively - Once you have built your audience, it is time to promote products effectively. This includes creating high-quality content that showcases the benefits of the products or services you are promoting and using call-to-actions to encourage your audience to make a purchase.

Step 4: Track your performance - To maximize your earnings, it is important to track your performance and make adjustments as needed. This includes tracking your click-through rates, conversion rates, and earnings per click.

Step 5: Build relationships with merchants - Building strong relationships with merchants can help you to negotiate higher commission rates and gain access to exclusive promotions and offers.

Affiliate marketing can be a highly profitable way to make money fast online. By choosing the right affiliate program, building your audience, promoting products effectively, tracking your performance, and building relationships with merchants, you can build a successful affiliate marketing business. In the next chapter, we will explore online courses and how you can use them to make money fast online.

Chapter 5

Online Courses

Online courses have become increasingly popular in recent years, and they provide a great opportunity for entrepreneurs and business owners to make money fast online. If you have expertise in a particular area, creating an online course can be a lucrative way to share your knowledge and skills with others. Here are some steps to help you create and sell online courses:

Step 1: Choose your topic and target audience - The first step in creating an online course is to choose your topic and target audience. You want to choose a topic that you are passionate about and that aligns with your skills and expertise. Additionally, you need to identify your target audience and their specific needs and pain points.

Step 2: Create your course content - Once you have chosen your topic and target audience, it is time to create your course content. This includes creating videos, written content, and other resources that provide value to your students.

Step 3: Choose a platform to host your course - There are many different platforms to choose from when it comes to hosting your online course, including Udemy, Teachable, and Kajabi. It is important to research different platforms to find one that meets your needs and budget.

Step 4: Market your course - To sell your online course, you need to market it effectively. This includes using social media marketing, content marketing, and email marketing to attract potential students to your course.

Step 5: Optimize your sales funnel - To maximize your sales, it is important to optimize your sales funnel. This includes creating effective landing pages, using email marketing to nurture your leads, and offering upsells and cross-sells to encourage students to buy more.

Creating and selling online courses can be a highly profitable way to make money fast online. By choosing the right topic and target audience, creating high-quality course content, choosing the right platform to host your course, marketing your course effectively, and optimizing your sales funnel, you can build a successful online course business.

Chapter 6

Freelancing

Freelancing is a flexible and profitable way to make money fast online. If you have skills in areas such as writing, design, programming, or virtual assistance, there are many opportunities to offer your services to clients online. Here are some steps to help you get started as a freelancer:

Step 1: Choose your niche - The first step in becoming a successful freelancer is to choose your niche. You want to choose an area that aligns with your skills and interests, and that has a demand for your services.

Step 2: Build your portfolio - To attract clients as a freelancer, you need to have a portfolio that showcases your skills and expertise. This includes creating high-quality samples of your work, testimonials from previous clients, and a professional website or online profile.

Step 3: Find clients - There are many different platforms to find clients as a freelancer, including Upwork, Freelancer, and Fiverr. Additionally, you can use social media and networking events to find potential clients.

Step 4: Set your rates - When it comes to setting your rates as a freelancer, it is important to consider your skills and experience, as well as the industry rates for your niche.

Step 5: Deliver high-quality work - To build a successful freelancing career, it is important to deliver high-quality work that meets your clients' needs and expectations.

Freelancing can be a great way to make money fast online, as long as you choose the right niche, build a strong portfolio, find clients effectively, set your rates competitively, and deliver high-quality work. In the next chapter, we will explore dropshipping and how you can use it to make money fast online.

Chapter 7

Dropshipping

Dropshipping is a popular e-commerce model that allows you to sell products online without having to hold inventory or manage shipping. Here are some steps to help you get started with dropshipping:

Step 1: Choose your niche - The first step in dropshipping is to choose your niche. You want to choose a niche that has a demand for your products, and that aligns with your interests and expertise.

Step 2: Choose a supplier - Once you have chosen your niche, you need to find a supplier who will provide the products you want to sell. You can find suppliers through online directories or by contacting manufacturers directly.

Step 3: Build your e-commerce store - To sell your products online, you need to build an e-commerce store. There are many different platforms to choose from, including Shopify, WooCommerce, and BigCommerce.

Step 4: Set your prices - When it comes to setting your prices, it is important to consider your profit margins and the prices of your competitors. You want to set prices that are competitive, but also allow you to make a profit.

Step 5: Market your products - To attract customers to your e-commerce store, you need to market your products effectively. This includes using social media marketing, content marketing, and email marketing to reach your target audience.

Step 6: Manage your orders and shipping - One of the benefits of dropshipping is that you don't have to manage inventory or shipping. Your supplier will handle the shipping and delivery of your products, but you still need to manage your orders and ensure that they are being fulfilled properly.

Dropshipping can be a profitable way to make money fast online, as long as you choose the right niche, find a reliable supplier, build a strong e-commerce store, set your prices competitively, market your products effectively, and manage your orders and shipping efficiently. In the next chapter, we will explore affiliate marketing and how it can help you make money fast online.

Chapter 8

Affiliate Marketing

Affiliate marketing is a popular way to make money fast online by promoting other people's products and earning a commission on the sales you generate. Here are some steps to help you get started with affiliate marketing:

Step 1: Choose your niche - The first step in affiliate marketing is to choose your niche. You want to choose a niche that has a demand for products, and that aligns with your interests and expertise.

Step 2: Find affiliate programs - Once you have chosen your niche, you need to find affiliate programs that offer products that are relevant to your niche. You can find affiliate programs through online directories or by contacting product owners directly.

Step 3: Build your audience - To promote products effectively as an affiliate marketer, you need to build an audience that trusts you and values your recommendations. This can include building a website, blog, social media following, or email list.

Step 4: Promote products - Once you have built your audience, you can start promoting products through your chosen channels. This can include creating product reviews, tutorials, and comparisons, or promoting products through social media posts and email newsletters.

Step 5: Track your results - To be successful in affiliate marketing, it is important to track your results and optimize your strategies based on what works best. This includes tracking your clicks, conversions, and earnings, and experimenting with different promotional methods.

Step 6: Stay up-to-date with trends and changes - Affiliate marketing is a dynamic field, and it is important to stay up-to-date with trends and changes in the industry. This includes staying informed about new products and services, changes in search engine algorithms, and updates to affiliate program policies.

Affiliate marketing can be a lucrative way to make money fast online, as long as you choose the right niche, find reliable affiliate programs, build a strong audience, promote products effectively, track your results, and stay up-to-date with trends and changes in the industry. In the next chapter, we will explore online courses and how you can use them to make money fast online.

Chapter 9

Creating Online Courses

Creating and selling online courses can be a profitable way to make money fast online. Here are some steps to help you get started with creating online courses:

Step 1: Choose your topic - The first step in creating online courses is to choose a topic that you are knowledgeable about and that has a demand in the market. You want to choose a topic that you are passionate about and that will appeal to your target audience.

Step 2: Plan your course - Once you have chosen your topic, you need to plan your course. This includes outlining the course content, deciding on the format of the course, and creating a syllabus.

Step 3: Create your course content - After planning your course, you need to create the content. This includes creating videos, slides, and other materials that will be included in the course.

Step 4: Choose a platform - To sell your course online, you need to choose a platform that will host your course. There are many different platforms to choose from, including Udemy, Teachable, and Thinkific.

Step 5: Set your price - When it comes to setting your price, it is important to consider the value of your course and the prices of similar courses in the market. You want to set a price that is competitive, but also reflects the value of your course.

Step 6: Market your course - To attract students to your course, you need to market it effectively. This includes using social media marketing, content marketing, and email marketing to reach your target audience.

Step 7: Get feedback and improve - After launching your course, it is important to get feedback from your students and use it to improve your course. This can include making updates to your course content or adjusting your marketing strategies.

Creating and selling online courses can be a profitable way to make money fast online, as long as you choose the right topic, plan your course effectively, create high-quality content, choose the right platform, set your price competitively, market your course effectively, and get feedback and improve over time. In the next chapter, we will explore freelancing and how it can help you make money fast online.

Conclusion

In conclusion, there are many different ways to make money fast online, including freelancing, e-commerce, affiliate marketing, and creating online courses. Each method requires a different set of skills, but they all share some common principles, such as choosing the right niche, building an audience, creating high-quality content, and marketing your products or services effectively. It is also important to stay up-to-date with trends and changes in the industry and to be willing to experiment and adapt your strategies based on what works best. With dedication, hard work, and a willingness to learn and grow, anyone can make money fast online and achieve financial independence. So, pick a method that aligns with your interests and strengths, and get started today!

www.ingramcontent.com/pod-product-compliance
Lightning Source LLC
Chambersburg PA
CBHW070854220526
45466CB00005B/1995